BOOK BENCHERS
PUBLICATIONS
PRESENTS

ENDLESS BEAUTY OF DIVINE

COMPILED BY -
SANJAY NAIK
MOHAMMED NIYAZ

BOOK BENCHERS

Book Benchers is the affiliate of Aelay publication.
Both the publication is handled by Astro.
Aelay plays the role of publishing solo books.
And Book Benchers is epically for publishing
anthologies.

Book Benchers have 2 different teams.
1. Tamil
2. English/Hindi

Never mind what our main motive is to help all the
budding writers, who are seeking for their dream of
publishing their own book to come true.

We are there to help out everyone.
In guiding for starting up with your carrier in
compiling until finishing up your full book.

ENDLESS BEAUTY OF DIVINE

<u>COPYRIGHT</u>

(Affiliate by Aelay Publish)

Book: ENDLESS BEAUTY OF DIVINE
Compiler: MOHAMMED NIYAZ
Compiler: SANJAY
First Edition: Augest 2021

Published By:
The Book Benchers
5/175, Fathima nagar,
Kuthenkuly,
Tirunelveli -627104
Phone: 9944992571

Design And Executed by

ISBN : 978-93-91423-78-0
Page : 123

<u>ACKNOWLEDGEMENT</u>

The day and the night has sun and moon for their cause, that's the inner beauty they hold on to with. Towards the almighty's blessings we can feel and experience the sources of bounties that differs among. **"Endless Beauty Of Divine"** under **Book Benchers Publication House** being **compiled** by **Sanjay Naik** And **Mohammed Niyaz** respectively. We are thankful to the **Founder Mr Astro Sir, the Team Head Miss. KA. Parina Sri** for having immense faith in us to compile this beautiful anthology. We are also thankful to our **"50 co-authors"** for pouring out their wonderful thoughts under this book. We hope our readers have a great time out there with the same.

<u>DISCLAIMER</u>

FOUNDER

IRUDAGA ASTRO

Irudaga Astro, From Tirunelveli, Founder of
Aelay and BB (Book Benchers)
He had completed his BE.
He has written 3 Tamil poetry book's which
hits the top list on social media!
His main aim is to allow the writers to
publish their words as their book rather than
just Posting them on Insta.

LINK AND POSTER MAKER

CATHERINE ASMI T

Catherine Asmi T, From Tirunelveli
She has completed her M.com
Her passion is Drawing and Designing.

Book Benchers

<u>TEAM HEAD</u>

She is a passionate writer from Chennai. Writing makes her pressure go away. She had played the role of co-author for more than 100+ Antho's. She would like to thank her parents and her Loveable Brother for supporting her rather than stopping her from what she wanted to do! For being the main reason for achieving her dreams. As well as for standing beside her in all the ups and downs. Whenever she feels like she needs to get out of her stressful timing or feels like she needs peacefulness, she starts to paint, she would never mind sitting in the same place for so many hours when it comes to her painting. She believes that anyone could hurt her, But never her books could!!

Catch her in Insta and FB
Insta: @theinnocentheart
FB: KA. PARINASRI

<u>INDEX</u>

27. ANKITA NAHAR
28. PRACHI GUPTA
29. ANANYA P MISHRA
30. MANSI SOLANKI
31. ROZY PAUL
32. TAHREEM AFZAL
33. ABDUR RAZZAQUE
34. NIDA J
35. UNNATI SAWANT
36. RAJESHWARI PANDIAN
37. ANKUR MISHRA
38. RAVISHANKER NISHAD (ARVI)
39. S.SUGANTHI
40. DAKSHITA JAISWAL
41. PRAKHAR RAGHUWANSHI
42. PRAKASH TURIYA (RAGHUWANSHI)
43. NAVEEN BHARDWAJ
44. TALIMA DAS
45. V.S.KAARTHIKVEL
46. GARGI GHOSH
47. SHIVANG SHARMA
48. SRIJITA SAHA
49. YOGESH GURJAR (CHINU)
50. ANUSHA SATHIA

ENDLESS BEAUTY OF DIVINE

SANJAY NAIK
(COMPILER)

Sanjay Naik is from Kharagpur State of West
Bengal. He is an Economics graduate (Hons), a
writer from the heart and passionate about singing.
Through the platform of anthology, he wants to
spread love & positivity among his readers and
wants to heal his readers' hearts with his magical
words. Sanjay is at utmost peace when he pens his
emotions. He believes that the power of his words,
will heal the wounds of many readers. Till now
participated in 200+ Anthologies as a CO-
AUTHOR. He is Compiler of anthology "SELF
HAPPINESS", "SCREAM" & " SARANG". And
now Compiled more than 50 + Anthologies.
Instagram:- @the_poetry_wo

<u>STAY CONNECTED !!</u>

Every person Collide someone in his life,
but believe that the absence of
which changes the color of your
face is something special.

You like to tease her, it is nice to be entangled in
her talk
You are neither aware of the time
nor your mind is ready to accept that
the moment spent with them is over.

Such people give a mark on the life path,
whose dealings are just with you
You decide this long journey with them
because you do not feel peace anywhere else.

ENDLESS BEAUTY OF DIVINE

MOHAMMED NIYAZ
(COMPILER)

मायानगरी मुंबई के रहने वाले मोहम्मद नियाज़ एक ड्रॉप-आउट इंजीनियरिंग स्टूडेंट है। शायरी की दुनिया में इनहोने अपना कदम साल २०१३ में रखा था। इनकी कई सारी शायरी फेसबुक और इंस्टाग्राम पर काफी मनोरंजीत करती है। यह भविष्य में एक राइटर बनना चाहते है। आप इनहे फेसबुक (Mohammed Niyaz) और इंस्टाग्राम (niyazsks) पर फॉलो कर सकते है।

<u>अदब-ए-किरदार</u>

हुस्न को सवारे तो चेहरे पर नज़र पढ़ी।
चेहरे को सवारे तो फिर कहीं जा कर अख़लाक़ पे बात आदि।

हालाकि हमने देखा है बसर को के
वह कुदरत के हिस्सों में से एक है।
समझ आया यह जान कर के
वह कई किस्सों है सबसे नेक है।

मगर फिर बात आयी उसस्के रवय्ये की।
तो भूले भटके कई रोज़माइये सी।

असर नामों निशानों तक नज़र रहा।
जहां तक होती उसकी पोहच चलता बसर रहा।

ना निगाहें फेरी ना ही कोई इलाज किया।
देखा एक दफा खुद को और फिर अंजाम-ए-राज़ किया।

कई बार चर्चों में आम-ए-ज़िन्दगी में रहा है।
मुक़म्मल जात और औकात की सीमा से बढ़ा है।

जान-ए-अंजाम से महज़ माना-ए-फर्मांबिरदार।
मशहूर क़ायनात की तौफ़ीक़ से "अदब-ए-किरदार"।

ENDLESS BEAUTY OF DIVINE

SHASWAT SOURAV SAHOO

Shaswat Sourav Sahoo, is an eighteen-something adventurer who grew up traversing the wonders through the pages of metaphors. He fell in love with books and never reverted. Today he is pursuing his studies and living a clichéd life at NISER as an Integrated M.Sc. research scholar. He has been recently awarded with the Global Achievers Award. When he is not surrounded by words you can spot him fancying and pampering the dogs. He is a jovial kind of person revamping his past grief events into allured moments. He loves voicing his emotions and get it penned down. Another feather to his cap is his intense intimacy with taking shots. Nevertheless, he is also impassioned for painting, playing indoors, origami. He is looking forward his life being a polymath and pour on whatever he possesses within and wishes never to quell it.

Instagram id - __shaswat__19

<u>BROKEN BUT ALIVE</u>

The emotions of my heart
Intangible and sharp
Drenched in the sea of
Grief making an arc

Sometimes taking the shape
Of angelica and Bholenath
Sometimes revamping into
Terence and god of wrath

Incomprehensible and unique
Juicy and sweet
Spicy and meat
Tasted these kit;
The emotions
Of My fragile heart

Broken but alive
Black but serene
Blunt deep inside still sharp
The emotions of my heart
Drap all the worthy feat
Nonetheless broken but Alive.

ENDLESS BEAUTY OF DIVINE

<u>ANAND JAIN</u>

ANAND JAIN is a good writer from FAZILKA,
PUNJAB
He has completed his GRADUATION in commerce
stream. From Panjab University.
He has been writing poetry for 4 years as his
passion.
He wants to be a successful banker in future.
He is a founder of ROBIN HOOD ARMY,
FAZILKA (NGO).
He is selected for the process of DEAR MOON
MISSION 2023

Instagram id - Anand_jain_12

चाहत तुम्हारी

अक्सर आँखे मूंद कर सोचा करता हूं तुम्हें
बंद आँखो से देख लेता हूं तुम्हें
शायद कुछ अनकही बातें आज भी बाकी है कहनी,
सोचकर उनको अकेले में ही मुस्कुराता हूं मैं..!

सोये हुए सपने आज भी जिंदा है जहन में मेरे
क्या उन पलों की आज भी उतनी ही एहमीयत है तुम्हे,
सोचा था उन सपनों को संजो कर रखूं यादों के धागों में,
पर आज भी तुम्हारे बिना अधूरा हूं मैं !!

कुछ अजीब सा कारवां चल रहा है यादों का
पास ना होकर भी महसूस कर रहा हूं तुम्हे,
काश तुम साथ होती अभी
ज़िंदगी को जान से भी ज्यादा चाहता मैं !!!

ENDLESS BEAUTY OF DIVINE

<u>VAISHNAWI KUMARI</u>

Vaishnawi kumari is from patna, Bihar.
She is a poetess, co-author and hindi writer.
She is studying as a computer science student in
NSIT BIHTA. Her hobbies are dancing, singing and
writing. She likes to decorate her feelings on a
paper.. She is motivated by her father.. She become
co-author of 150+ successful anthologies with
different publications and 10+ world record
Anthologies. And now she is working as a author of
4 Anthologies with different publications. If you
want to connect with her personally then follow her
Instagram handle @kumarivaishnawi and for her
quote and poetry then follow @mystic.vaishu

A MOMENT

Some memories of bygone moments,
And when they come, they moisten their eyes,
I think sometimes how beautiful those moments
were,
When you and I were close to each other,
Can't describe that happy moment,
What we and you spent with each other,
People change in this world,
But their memories remain
And with the help of those memories, we also cut
our lives,
We both have similar memories too.
With which till today,
I feel very comfortable in myself,
No matter how much I try,
But can't bring that moment back,
There is one thing in this mind,
I can't forget those moments.....

<u>HAR DEEPANSH BAHADUR SINHA</u>

He is Har Deepansh Bahadur Sinha .
He belongs to Lucknow,UP.
He is a research scholar of Oceanography and has
done masters in Geography from National Post
Graduate College.
Completed his schooling from Study Hall.
His hobbies are art , listening to music , cooking &
loads of driving.
His interest areas are Astronomy, Writing,
Photography & Travelling a lot.

Instagram id - Deepansh_sinha

<u>MY FIRST PROPOSAL</u>

I was single by my choice
Happy and lost in my voice,
Not in hurry affection
Far away from relations.

I was enjoying my college life
Came in contact with my future wife,
It was the season of chilled winters
She knocked my heart and wanted to enter.

For the first time I felt for a girl
She was alluring just like a pearl,
Days passed away we came closer
I got extremely phenomenal exposure.

One day she suddenly proposed
For her my love got exposed,
Her eyes were reflecting devotion
And her lips showed emotions.

A brand new journey got started
Literally she is very kind hearted,
Now I was completely caged
Since we both got engaged.

ENDLESS BEAUTY OF DIVINE

My first proposal was my last
Everytime she turned my beats fast,
So finally we tied the knot
Believe me stars has no fault.

PRIYA SINGH

Priya Singh is born & brought up in Dewas,
MadhyaPradesh.She's a Proud daughter if her Father
B.N.Singh (T.I.).She's completed Masters of Computer
Science.She is a Former Educationist, Communication Trainer
& Avid Reader.
She's the Co-Author of the Anthologies:-
"It's all about two phase : love & hate" ,"Words From Heart",
"Fierce, Fearless N Flawed" & "In the way of borehole",
"Unseen Blessings & "Sublime Love", "Mere Papa".
All are available in Amazon.
Till today, She's worked in 200+ Anthologies as a Co-Author
& compiling 3.
Her writing keeps her at ease.
She mostly write quotes on thoughts.
She loves inspiring young minds.
Instagram id- instant__thoughts_

ENDLESS BEAUTY OF DIVINE

Energy hidden in a soul
seeking something as goal,
there's purpose of everything
that comes on the globe,
until you accomplish it,
you would never cherish life
Whole.

You've fire within
that keeps you going
until you get it,
you won't go that
far you supposed to.

A string of hope
is enough as rope
to go on while
stinging with negative
thoughts though,
it's a spark that ignites
soul with immense
happiness & energy
as goal to achieve.

MADHUMITA

A conscious dreamer letting her thoughts out
through pen and paper

Instagram id - Feel.Free.Fun.24

ENDLESS BEAUTY OF DIVINE

<u>POSITIVITY</u>

Positivity comes from within,
It endow happiness and love spin.

Positivity comes from within,
awaken our soul to talk with upright chin.

It creates energy when we think,
it attract thoughts and merge in a wink.

If you think bad for others,
it perceive as your own errors.

So beware of your thoughts and actions,
it create energy and momentum in fractions.

If you think good,
it creates happiness and not misunderstood.

So prosperity can't buy you peace,
only you can think and get it at ease.

You are responsible to what you own,
your thoughts adds adjectives to your noun.

So love and pamper yourself,
You will get what you deserve my elf.

Positivity always comes from within,
Only love can cleanse your heart to twain.

MOHD. FARHAN ALAM LARI

Hello, I am Mohd.Farhan Alam Lari. I am from Bahraich,UP. I am a strong believer in the benevolence of God. I have trained my eyes on having completed my post-graduation in commerce, I am now keen on cracking the various competitive examinations. And i believe the best way to convey one's thoughts is by the medium of poems. This has inspired me to explore the literary world. I secured the position of "2nd_Runner_Up" in my first online competition held by "RJ Academy in August-2020". I won many "Daily and Weekly poetry challenges" on different social media platforms. I have also got the title of "Writer of the Week and Writer of the Month". I got the opportunity to Co-Author in "40+Anthologies". Since April 2021, I have been Compiling "5-books". n i will forever grateful for your love and Cooperation....

Instagram id - funkaar_farhan.lari

<u>"बचपन की यादें,कोई लौटा दे!"</u>

आओ सुनाता हूँ, बचपन की कहानी!
जब हम सब करते थे, खूब मनमानी!!

काश! कोई हो जो, हमें लौटा दे!
हमारी बचपन की, वो हसीन यादें!!

जब बचपन में हम सब, रहते थे एक साथ!
बस हर वक़्त करते थे, खेलने की ही बात!!

वो हम सबका मिलकर, एक साथ खाना!
स्कूल न जाने का, ढूँढना कोई बहाना!!

गलती करने पर, माँ का हमें समझाना!
फिर प्यार से हमें, देखकर मुस्कुराना!!

पापा का शाम को, घर वापस आना!
आते ही उनको, प्यार से गले लगाना!!

हम भाई-बहनों से, आपस में करते थे लड़ाई!
मगर साथ में ही खाते, और करते थे पढ़ाई!!

वो स्कूल में बेंच के लिये, आपस की लड़ाई!
कभी-कभी दोस्तों ने, पिटाई भी करवाई!!

वो हम सबका एक साथ, कही पर घूमने जाना!
वापस आकर एक-दूसरे को, वहाँ की हर बार बताना!!

वो बचपन में, भाई-बहनों का हर वक़्त साथ!
बड़े होने पर क्यूँ? छोड़ देते एक-दूसरे का हाथ!!

ऐसे ही है बचपन की, बहुत सारी यादगार बातें!
जिन्हें अब सोचकर ही, हम सब है खूब मुस्कुरातें!!

काश! फिर लौट आये, वो बचपन के पल!
जो रह गये बनके, सिर्फ एक हसीन पल!!

PAYAL KAMDI

Payal Kamdi from Maharashtra.
A girl with passion in writing mess with her heart and mind.The picking of ink and fell down of paper which comes along shadow. She is penning her thoughts by pen name Nityashree. She believes writing helps to concrete thoughts and manifest faster. Being a self lover she is binder of relationships too.
Love can loose you but gives you hope of finding stars, she convinced.

Book Benchers

I met him in my dreams
I never thought to fall in love
I was at point to fell for beauty only
Once again I met in dreams
he started to talked with me
his voices touches me
he was like inspirational note of life
he touches my soul before body
as soon as I saw him
he was not like a moon
but not less than everything
finally my heart beats for his soul
more than beauty of face
his rhyme matches true beauty.

KALAMKAAR

इनका नाम कलमकार है ये उत्तराखंड के रहने वाले है , मगर मेरठ में रह रहे हैं ! इनको लिखना और पढ़ना पसंद है! इन्होने 860+ अन्थोलॉजी में सेह लेखक के रूप में काम किया है और 740+ सम्मान पत्र जीते है! इनको लिखना और पड़ना पसंद है!इनकी रूचि लिखने में है!इनको कर्म पर विश्वास है फल से ज्यादा! इन्होने 20+पुस्तक में भाग लिया है सह लेखक के रूप में जो रिकॉर्ड के लिए गयी है!

Instagram id - Kalamkaar51

<u>बुरा ख़्याल ना आने दे</u>

हार जाये अगर ज़िन्दगी में कभी तो खुदको कमज़ोर ना समझे!
सोचकर खुदको अवसाद में ना जाने दे
ये तो सिर्फ एक पहलु है ज़िन्दगी है!
बुरा ख्याल ना आने दे!
हार कर फिर जीत मिल सकती है दोबारा!
हार हालातो के आगे खुदको ना मानने दे!
लड़े फिर से और जीते फिर से एक योद्धा की तरह!
और बुरा ख्याल ना आने दे!
ठोंकर खाकर ही आदमी कुछ सीखता है!
सकारात्मक सोच रखे और अपने अंदर आने दे!
बुरे ख्यालो आपके ज़ेहन में कभी ना आये!
बुरा ख़्याल ना आने दे!
सबसे खुदको सर्वश्रेष्ठ माने हमेशा से!
कमज़ोर मानकर खुदको किसी से यूँही ना हारने दे!
लड़े जबतक जीत आपकी नहीं हो जाती!
और बुरा ख़्याल ना आने दे!

HARSHITA VERMA

Co-author Harshita Verma is a writer from Lucknow. She has completed her graduation in commerce stream. She has been writing poetry for the last few years as her passion. She wants to be a novelist in future.

Instagram id - 0___hsh

<u>WEDDING</u>

A beautiful day it is
Flowers and beauty present
Happiness and joy of people
The most happy bride and groom

A trip to the wedding
The feast for all loved ones
The tying of knot for the future
Enjoying each moment of the phase

The music softest
Making the mind go with flow
The beautiful decoration of area
Catching the hearts whoever saw
The best day in life the wedding day

ENDLESS BEAUTY OF DIVINE

<u>MANISHA S KAUSHAL</u>

इनका नाम मनीषा कौशल है। झीलों की नगरी भोपाल की ये रहने वाली है। वर्तमान में ये श्री भवंस भारती पब्लिक स्कूल में हिंदी शिक्षिका के पद पर कार्यरत हैं। इन्हें लिखने का शौक बचपन से था परन्तु अपने शौक को कभी व्यक्त नहीं किया। कोरोना काल के अन्तर्गत मन में बसी हुई सारी बातें इन्होंने लेखन के द्वारा व्यक्त की। पिछले 15 वर्षों से ये बच्चों को हिंदी पढ़ाती आ रही है। लेखन क्षेत्र में ये और लिखना चाहती है।

Instagram id - Manisha Kaushal75

"मेरे पिता"

तुलात्मक अध्ययन कभी मैने मेरे पिता में नहीं पाया
क्योंकि उनकी नज़रों में सदा मैने खुद को श्रेष्ठ है पाया,
तेरह वर्ष के होते ही मै बड़ी हो गई, सबकी नज़रों में
चूल्हा - चौंका संभालने योग्य हो गई,
थी थोड़ी पढ़ने में कमज़ोर इसलिए सबका मुंह बनता था,
विद्यालय का परिणाम देख सबका क्रोध उफनता था,
बस एक साया ऐसा था जो सदा सुरक्षित रखता था,
उनके पास जाकर ही तो सुकून सबसे अधिक मिलता था,
सांवली होने पर भी सबसे अधिक प्यारी थी मै,
मेरे पिता की राजदुलारी थी मै
हौसला देते रहे मुझको, हताश ना कभी होना
इस दुनिया का काम ही है बेटा सबकी टांग खिंचना
सीखा गए इस जग में रहना अपनी फूल कुमारी को
नहीं हार मानना कभी चाहे कैसी भी हों परिस्थिति...

ENDLESS BEAUTY OF DIVINE

<u>SHIVAM MAURYA</u>

इनका नाम :~ शिवम् मौर्या
यह गोरखपुर उत्तर प्रदेश से हैं।
ये दिल से एक लेखक और गायन के बारे में भावुक।
वह अपने पाठकों के बीच प्यार और सकारात्मकता
फैलाना चाहता है और अपने जादुई शब्दों से अपने
पाठकों के दिलों पर मरहम लगाना चाहता है।
शिवम सबसे ज्यादा शांतमय है
उनका मानना है कि उनके शब्दों की शक्ति, कई पाठकों
के घावों को ठीक कर देगी।

Instagram id - @_as___writes_

बहुत रो लिए जिन्दगी मे ,
चलो हंसने की कोई
एक नई वजह ढूंढते हैं ।।

बहुत रह लिए ग़म में ,
चलो जहां ग़म न हो
ऐसी एक नई वजह ढूंढते हैं ।।

उड़ तो बहुत लिए ऊंचे गगन ,
चलो जमीं पे कहीं
एक नहीं सतह ढुंढते है ।।

साथ छोड़ा बहुतों ने जिन्दगी की सफर में ,
चलो दिल से सब भुला कर
एक नई साथी ढूंढ़ते हैं ।।

बहुत वक़्त गुज़रा खुद कि तलाश में ,
चलो आईने के सामने खड़े होकर
खुद में कोई नई कमी ढूंढते हैं ।।

ENDLESS BEAUTY OF DIVINE

<u>LIPSA DABHI</u>

She is lipsa dabhi. She is Author and also good Co-Author. She is eighteen years old, she is student of the computer engineering.She is extraordinary person. She is always good leader. Her mam mrunal prajapati is her inspiration person and also her motivator, her friend chetna raval also supported to her and her mom manisha ben and her father nilesh bhai also supported to her for anytype of her creativity.
she also wrote poems, short stories, shayaris.
Her writing skills are almost very well and her creative collections are always best.

Instagram id - __lipsa__dabhi__0829

" TRUST "

Trust is precious part of life,
Also trustful life is best but with loyalty,
Trust is gift from god and Trust is unique part of
life.

Sometimes someone's trust is most important part of
us life,
Because someone is most important in your life and
you never miss trust him/her. Trust is powerful tool
and also expensive.

Never brake anyone's trust because of trust is extra
important in life,
Trust is one time only added us but next time
learned us never trust to anyone

ENDLESS BEAUTY OF DIVINE

" EDUCATION IS PRECIOUS "

Education is the pillar of our society,
Education is the way of success,
Education is the good way,
And education is perfect part for ur life.

Educate people deserved more success,
And always more achievements,
Education is very important to us,
Education is the password to the future.

Education is the great opportunity for all human,
Education is same for all people,
Education is not for anyone person,
but education is our.

ABHISHEK SINGH PARCHA

अभिषेक सिंह पर्चा ये 12वीं पास है और ये स्टेनोग्राफी विद्यार्थी हैं
इन्हें लिखना बेहद पसंद है, ये दिल्ली के कमल पार्क में रहते हैं ये रैपर लिरिक्स और कविता करते हैं । इन्हें लिखने की प्रेरणा डॉ. राहत इंदौरी साहब से मिली है

Instagram id - Abhishek_singh_parcha

ENDLESS BEAUTY OF DIVINE

मेरा दिल हर बार तोड़ा गया है
ना जाने उसे कही बार उसे जोड़ा गया है
तोफा तो उसने मुझे बहुत बेमिसाल दिया है
अपनी वफा का जिसमें मुझे बेवफा का इल्जाम दिया है।

#अभिषेक
(अभिषेक सिंह पर्चा)

गुस्सा वो ऐसे करती है जैसे वो मुझे मार ही डालेगी।
पर जरा सी चोट भी लग तो वो आसमान को सिर पर
उठा लेगी।
वो कोई और नहीं मेरी मां है जो मुझसे प्यार तो बहुत
करती है पर जताती नहीं

#अभिषेक
(अभिषेक सिंह पर्चा)

अच्छा हुआ था वो मुझे छोड़ कर चली गई थी
वो बेवफा थी मगर उसने वफा अच्छी की थी
मैं दोहराता हू वो किससे अपनी शायरी में
जिसे वह अधूरा छोड़ गई थी।

ANKITA MISHRA

I am Ankita Mishra from Cuttack, Odisha. I am a student pursuing my graduation in bachelor's of commerce. Writing was never my passion nor my hobby. All I loved was singing, crafting and playing badminton. Then when I used to stay alone I used to write my feelings no matter happy or sad. And that's how I started writing by expressing my thoughts, feelings and emotions into words. I just hope and look forward towards taking this habit as my passion.

Instagram id - @the_imperfect_writer_08

ENDLESS BEAUTY OF DIVINE

I saw a beautiful dream,
where there were just you and me.
In a small little world,
where lived were just we.

There was no more pain,
only happiness that we gained.
After all the struggles that we faced,
in our entire journey's way.

Everything seemed to be worth it,
when we together did it.
It's our unity that made it happen,
after crossing every situation.

Our understanding made us accept,
every hurdles that came our way.
Our communication made us cross,
every stoned pathway.

Where there was no restriction,
without any caste discrimination.
We lived happily ever after
let's go that dream nation.

As a vehicle can't move
without its wheels,
So as we is incomplete
without you and me.

<u>LIZA PATEL</u>

23 साल की कॉन्फिडेंट गर्ल लीजा पटेल। उसकी इच्छा अपनी सारी भावनाओं, सारी दुनिया में खुशी का संचार करना है। पेशे से एक इंजीनियर के रूप में कई चीजें सीखीं और अपनी सभी यादें साझा करना शुरू कर दिया। मूल रूप से उसका प्रयास है कि सभी दिल से लिखें और जुड़े।

Instagram id - @liza_quotes

<u>तेरे मधुर वचन को हमेशा मैं सुनता रहूँ</u>

तेरे मधुर वचन को हमेशा मैं सुनता रहूँ
अपनी बातों को मैं तेरे दर रखु
तू जो है मेरा रक्षक
तू जो है मेरा साथी
तू जो है मेरा स्वामी
तू जो है मेरा प्राणप्रिय

जब जब मैं था अकेला
भर दिया तूने अपने रुह से
कारगार बनाता है तू हर काम मेरे
जब मैं जाता हूँ तेरे सम्मुख

गाता हूँ मैं तेरा नाम
प्रशंसा मैं करता हूँ तेरी सुबह शाम
तेरी महिमा का वर्णन
सुनाता रहूँगा मैं हर दम

<u>DEEPANSHI GUPTA</u>

Deepanshi gupta is of 20 years. Recently she completed her graduation. She is from saharanpur uttar pradesh. She is not a professional writer. Its her hobby. She likes to express her feelings and thoughts in form of shayaris and poetries. She got this inspiration of writing from her parents. She want to do something great in this field and want to achieve name with fame from this inspiring field of writing.

Good luck dear🩶

Instagram id - Mann_ke.alfaaz

ENDLESS BEAUTY OF DIVINE

मैं ज़िंदगी में कुछ अलग करना चाहती हुँ,
कोई बनना चाहता है डॉक्टर ,
या कुछ उससे भी बड़ा,
लेकिन मैं एक ऐसा इंसान बनना चाहती हुँ,
जो ख़ामोशी में छिपे लफ्ज़ों को पढ़ सके,
जो मुस्कुराती आँखों से गमो को देख सके,
जो किसी डूबती कश्ती का सहारा बन सके,
जो किसी बहती नदी का किनारा बन सके,
जिससे मिलकर हो किसी की तलाश पुरी,
मैं एक ऐसा इंसान बनना चाहती हुँ,
मैं ज़िंदगी में कुछ अलग करना चाहती हुँ।।

दिपांशी गुप्ता

ANMOL CHUGH DILDARD

Anmol Chugh Dildard is a student of civil engineering at St. Soldier group of institutions. He is from Jalandhar City, Punjab. He is love to read and write thoughts and poetry.He has participated in many books. He has compiled a contribution book " Tere Rubaroo". He has recently compiled his solo book " वास्तविकता"

Instagram id - anmolchugh8383

"इंसानियत"

इंसान भी आज इंसान से कहता है,
जानवरों पर विश्वास करो,
लेकिन मुझे माफ करो,
मेरा ना विश्वास करो।
मैं इंसानियत के जितने भी पन्ने पढ़ा हूं,
सब अपनी मां से पढ़ा हूं सीखा हूं।
मेरी मां का कहना है,
कि जहां इंसानियत जिंदा है,
वहां धर्म की कोई बात नहीं होती,
और जहां पैसे की बात हो,
वहां इंसानियत की कोई औकात नहीं होती।

AMIT KUMAR

मेरा नाम अमित कुमार है मैं बीएचयू के मेडिकल डिपार्टमेंट में सेकंड ईयर का छात्र हूं मैंने लिखना 2017 से शुरू किया ।मैंने सच्चा लेख अपनी मित्र के साथ से सीखा है

Instagram id - yashit9598

ENDLESS BEAUTY OF DIVINE

मैं जब भी लिखता हूं,
थोड़ा संभल कर लिखता हूं,
दिमाग से कम दिल से ज्यादा लिखता हूं
इतना बेशकीमती कागज जो है,
हर सस्ती महंगी चीजों पर,
सबसे पहले तेरा नाम लिखता हूं
फूलों के नाम लिखता हूं,
आशिकों के अल्फाज लिखता हूं
है ख्वाहिश ख्वाबों की
मैं क्या करता हूं,
खुशबू की बाजार से
महकता सा पैगाम लिखता हूं,
कभी राम लिखता हूं
कभी अल्लाह लिखता हूं
जब थक जाता हूं
तेरा ही नाम लिखता हूं,
ना स्याही खत्म होती है
ना ही कलम थक कर रूकती है
ना सिलसिला थमता है
ना कहानी यह खत्म होती है,
मानो समुंदर में रिमझिम बरसात होती है
खुदा जानता है
यह उसकी मर्जी से ही है,
इसलिए मैं अपने खुदा का नाम लिखता हूं

SONAL PRAJAPATI

I am Sonal Prajapati living in Delhi. Electrical Engineer by profession and writer by passion. I had been part of online writing contest and books like the cage of soul, jeevansathi, the inked solace, classy lassie, hope- a positive vibes, colleen warriors, soliloquy, twinkling versus, Nzare unke, love is everything, Incarnation and hope- faith & trust, love-a journal, friendship a book, kuch lamhe yaadon ke , satrangi barsaat , ishq ke raste, lines from the heart, Tu jo mere sath hai

Instagram id - Misswriter_

ENDLESS BEAUTY OF DIVINE

In a world of full confusion
You are the one which is my compulsion
I carry all my desire
Because I want to be your fire
Having your hug in a day
It is like a shower in month of may
You carry my stuff all the time
Your every words matches words of mine
Your heart pumps thinking about me
Only this thing I can see, see, see
You are a true blessing to my life
I really really want to be your wife.

<u>SRIJA SADHUKHAN</u>

Srija Sadhukhan is 19 years old girl studying BSc Biotechnology in Amity University Kolkata. Love to write poetry and a book worm too.

Instagram id - Syncopatemysuccess

<u>ADDICTION</u>

Addiction is the worst drug itself
The world is full of fake friends
With that I started taking drugs
Losing my attention and concentration
Friends influenced and drug became my habit.
Craving for drug spoiled my life
Parents had unbelievable faith on me
By friends spoiled my present
And my studies in abroad life also spoiled
Drug habitation chewed my relations.
I lost everything I had in my life
My life is in pain and addiction,
When nothing was in my hand
I realized to fight against my addiction.
Ten years of rehabilitation cured me up
I got rid of drug
But it ruined my whole life.
I lost my parents in this tenure.
I lost everything in this addiction.

BERDHISHA P

Berdhisha is from Tamil Nadu. She is a poet who loves to share her own thoughts and imagination. Furthermore, she loves to write and read novels. She is a blogger (berdhisha96.), Co-author for about 60+ Anthologies and a compiler too. She loves nature, which is her best friend.

Instagram id - thoughts_of_mine_the_muse

ENDLESS BEAUTY OF DIVINE

<u>QUOTES</u>

Love is unconditional,
When it comes beyond status,
When it comes beyond race,
And when it comes beyond everything.

Love all with your beautiful heart,
Trust some with your wonderful heart,
Arise question in all situation,
With your brilliant mind.

Money gives you status
Money creates a great environment
But people are fake,
They get close with you only for your money.

In ancient times, earned money
Even after retirement
But nowadays earning money
And getting retirement earlier.

Sea waves reach the shore,
It kisses every time,
Never get bored to touch
And kiss the feet of shore.

When someone seeks your help,
Help them with all your heart,
Because, though they had a confidence on you,
They seek help to you.

SONALI MEHER

Hey readers....!! She is Sonali Meher. From - Nuapada, Odisha, India. Currently pursuing for the degree of BAMS at Sri Sri nursingnath ayurveda medical College and RI. She is a Doctor by profession and writer by passion. She started writing when a very special moments come in her life and now for her writing is hobby. The writing is the 3rd person in that way of expressing their feelings, emotions and love. Now get a platform to exploring her writing. Hope ! You guys like it.

Instagram id - Sonalimeher124

ENDLESS BEAUTY OF DIVINE

पहली बार जब आपको मिले थे हम सोचे भी नहीं थे ।
आप हमारी ज़िन्दगी मैं ऐसे खुशियां भर देंगे ।
आपके साथ जितना भी लम्हा गुजारू कम हैं ।
और थोड़ी देर साथ रहने की दिल होता हैं ।

सब तो हमारी बात सुन ते है समझ ते भी हैं ।
पर आप बो बात को मेहेसुस करते हैं ।
मोहब्बत कैसे हुआ क्यू हुआ पता नहीं ।
बस आपसे हैं और आपसे ही रहेगा बो पता हैं ।

दिन मैं जब भी आपकी याद आती है ।
आपकी तस्वीर को देखकर दिल को सुकून आता हैं ।
दूर होके भी हम दोनों दिल के पास ही हैं।
हम दोनों पास होने का महसूस करते हैं ।

आपसे दूर जाने से अछा हैं हम मर ही जाएं
आपके लिए दुनिया भी छोड़ देंगे ।
मेरे दिल की बस एक ख्वाहिश हैं ।
आप हमेशा खुश रहे और मेरे साथ रहे ।

<u>AKKSHAYA PRASANNA</u>

Gracious smile, Anxious heart,conscious mind

Instagram id - Akkshaya_prasanna_JK

ENDLESS BEAUTY OF DIVINE

Where does the beauty lies ,
The beauty lies in eyes
Who see nice in others
Not their wealth,outer appearance
But their capability
out of their disability

Where does the beauty lies ,
The beauty lies in eyes
Who see that they are discouraged
but encourage themselves to move
This is ability of their hard work
Beyond capabilities

Where does the beauty lies
The beauty Lies in eyes
Who have pimple shield
to hide their face
like pine have hard skin
But they are sweet as
Pulp in pine

Where does the beauty lies
The beauty lies in the eyes
Who smile for rejections
Smile for discouragement
Smile for depression
And thus real beauty
Lies on smile and not
The colour of lipstick

Real beauty is an endearing one.

<u>DHARSHINI.M</u>

She is dharshini from kovilpatti. She is pursing masters in English. She has huge interest in writing.she loves to share her thought and emotion through her writing.She has done many anthologies as co author . She has published a book named 'vox of mine '.

Instagram id - dharshji_dharsh

ENDLESS BEAUTY OF DIVINE

<u>QUOTES</u>

Though you lose your money
Though you lose your things
It doesn't affect much
Don't lose your mind and heart
It's affects you high

Beauty remains today
Money remains now
But loyal heart remains strong forever

Endless love feel ensure the care
Endless care ensure the love
Both are interconnected strongly.

My dear darling
You are born to shine
Be a warrior to fight hard
For your dreams

Cry hard, be alone
Whenever you feel low
It's doesn't matter
How fast you bounce back from it matters!!

ANJALI SAMUNDRE

Anjali!! I'm from jabalpur mp. I'm in 19. I studying now b.com last year. I. Started writing last 5 years. I really like to write & read. My first write-up for my world, my lovely mother.

Instagram id - The_unbeatable_girl

<u>पसंद</u>

उसको जब मैने पहली बार देखा,
मुझे वो दीदार पसंद हैं।
वो जो तू किसी और को देखकर मुझसे टकराई,
मुझे वो तकरार पसंद हैं।
वो तेरा नाजुक होने पर भी दबंगई दिखाना, मेरे सामने
आते ही शांत हो जाना,
मुझे वो तेरा रूप पसंद हैं।
वो तेरा बात-बात में मुँह फुलाना, मुझे देखकर छिप जाना,
मैं तेरे करीब आऊं तो तेरा शर्माना और तेरा यूँ मुझे स्पर्श
करके जाना,
हां मुझे तेरी ये शरारत पसंद हैं।
वो तेरा इठलाना, बलखाना, कभी-कभी बच्ची से बन
जाना,वो तेरा मुस्कुराना, वो तेरा आँख दिखाना,
हां मुझे तेरी ये अदा भी पसंद हैं।
हाँ मुझे वो शख्श पसंद हैं जिसने मुझे अपनी आंखों,
अपनी बातों,अपनी सांसों, अपनी मुलाकातों का दीवाना
बनाया हैं।
हां मुझे वो पसंद हैं।।

ANKITA NAHAR

#AKII#@@@
Ankita Nahar, physically she live in AJMER,
RAJASTHAN but heartly live in everywhere.
She is too much passionate about writing.
She have always found comfort in words, and thats
what attracts everyone.Writing is her therapy, she
write what she feels and experiences in her life. You
can take a look at her writings on Instagram
@naharankita1

ENDLESS BEAUTY OF DIVINE

Go to her in marriage
and be able to see it,
this is my wish
I wish I could complete it.

that husband is mine
I'll be his wife
this is my wish
I wish I could complete it.

seven births not right
I will be her in this birth
this is my wish
I wish I could complete it.

His name behind my name Next to the children's
name His name
this is my wish
I wish I could complete it.

yes when my last time
With that time I will also find yours
this is my wish
I wish I could complete it.

PRACHI GUPTA

Prachi Gupta is a Passionate writer who loves to create her imaginary arts in a random canvas. She is pursuing her studies in BBA and lives in Allahabad known as The pure city of Sangam.

She loves to sing and watching movies in her free time.
She is a shy and a open-minded girl at the same time

For more information can follow her and contact:-
Prachiguptt0210@gmail.com
Instagram id - @prachigupta3435
@prachi_gupta_210

ENDLESS BEAUTY OF DIVINE

<u>NOISE</u>

What is this noise of?
Cause it effects peace
Or disturbs your week

What is this Scold of?
Cause it changes the behaviour
Or silent your Angry mood

What is this insult of?
Cause it shows the class
Or satisfy your high needs

What is this jealousy of?
Cause you are afraid to loss
Or you wanna make your standard more splendid
than others

What is this chaos of?
Can't it be Shut Off??

<u>ANANYA P MISHRA</u>

She is a girl with lot of patience and as calm as sea her name is Ananya P Mishra from Bhubaneswar, Odisha. She is completing her graduation in English Honors. Bedside that an Interior designer. She has been an active participant in literary arts, competitions.

<u>THE CREATOR -</u>

The path trending which a man sees himself as a
soul and knows himself to be a fragment of God,
That path is called Justice.
When a man knows himself to be a fragment of God
he has an epiphany that creation is God and God is
creation.
There's no difference between creation and God.

<u>MANSI SOLANKI</u>

Mansi Solanki from Navsari, Gujarat. She is currently pursing diploma civil engineering from Uka Tarsadia university. She have started writing a month ago and she loves to write poems, shayari, quotes, one liner. She is CoAuthor of 30+ anthologies and thank you for giving her chance for this anthology.

Instagram id - @inked_solace26

ENDLESS BEAUTY OF DIVINE

She's a perfect mess
She is a combination of
Heavenly smile,
Deadly eyes,
Wild heart,
Kid at mind..,
And live a life with a
Free spirit,
Happy soul,
Calm mind.
She's a perfect mess,
A beautiful calamity,
Chaos within tragedy.

<u>ROZY PAUL</u>

Her name is Rozy Paul.She belongs to the tea-estate
called Dibrugarh,Assam.She has done M.A.in
journalism.Her hobbies are reading,gardening and
cooking.She likes travelling a lot.Her favourite
quote is 'live and let live'.

Instagram id - writer_rozypaul

<u>ADVISE</u>

People easily and interestingly started giving advise to others. Do that or do this,don't do that,for elder persons make this very annoying.That is superior tendency when you learn from others just practice it when you know everything then give advise to others. Submissive people rare to give advise others their behaviour bounds others to follow them.That is really a person's endless beauty."

<u>TAHREEM AFZAL</u>

She has done her MS in Mathematics. Besides being a dream hunter, she is the girl who is traveling on the path called 'life'. She doesn't complain for the obstacles, she just makes sure that her faith never gets blurry, as this is the only candle of light which keeps her going in dark nights.

Instagram id - Reemsays789

ENDLESS BEAUTY OF DIVINE

THE ONLY HEALER

~Trouble arises when the person, who gave you
deepest scars, starts to appear like your only cure.
Trouble was not that
she couldn't get the healer.
Trouble was that
the person who gave her scars
was appearing to be
her only healer too.

HER MESSY EXISTENCE

She had everything in her
that could make her unwanted.
She was the queen of
some amend-less flaws and ugly scars.
With some bitter truths as a part of her,
she could never think to be loved
even like an ordinary girl.
People wanted the flower
which could only bloom in their yard,
but she knew how to bloom
even on barren land.
She was like a dark cloud
which could only offer the thunder,
in a world where people hailed
the clouds showering rain.

Book Benchers

Then one day,
when she felt completely alienated,
she started to get the love
from a person who loved the imperfections.
With each passing day,
he proved to her that
she was not a mess
that couldn't be made part of home.
Instead, she was a mess
that could be made part of another messy soul,
beautifully completing each other
without settling for perfections and cleanness.
Indeed, she was a mess
that could only be handled by him,
the owner of an even messier soul,
who saw the beauty in her flaws,
who saw the perfection in her imperfection.

ABDUR RAZZAQUE

Abdur Razzaque has been writing passionately since High School and currently working on his poems collection along with being a co-author in various anthologies since last year. After graduating in English literature, he started writing on regular basis.

He always says, "A writer lives in another dimension, you just see a glimpse of him."

Instagram id - strangebuttruequotes

DESTRUCTION HAS A FACE

Let's talk about us, humanity, these days,
We're just idols, useless things, with no humanity
left.
Behaving chaotically, hence sharing the same rays.
Races end, species entincting, like our souls has
been theft.

We want peace, but breaks everything in pieces,
Created only chaos, war, hatred and only
destructions.
Killing innocents, being egoistic, everything we
ceases,
And those so called netizens, scream it aloud, not
showing any actions.

Deforestation, global warming, slowly increasing,
Yet we talk about those stupid movie reviews.
Terrorism and mob-lynching, just trying to defame
the Holy,
Most of us hate it, but a few stays silent, point of
views.

Ashamed of these phantom memories, not proud,
Let's stop this nuisance, I screamed it aloud.
Abdur Razzaque

ENDLESS BEAUTY OF DIVINE

<u>NIDA J</u>

Nida J, is a Writer, Blogger, Co-author of more than 50
anthologies and an aspiring author. She likes books, coffee and
literature.
Her journey started when she wrote her first poem about
Women Empowerment, in class eight. Writing
makes flowers bloom in her
heart; flowers, that can help,
heal and inspire people to reform.
She likes to learn not only things that would help her
achieve her goal but also people, she likes listening to
people's stories which helps her see the world from their
eyes. Her favorite genres are romance and motivation not just
for reading but writing as well. You can find her blog at
www.ajeelicewits.wordpress.com
You can also contact her @nidaaaj24@gmail.com

<u>OH LOVE !</u>

Oh love! I wanna write odes for you
About your hair that dances with the wind
And about those eyes that are deep blue.

Oh love! I want to write poems for you
Describing every inch of your skin
Describing it in ways, you never knew.

Oh love! I want to address letters to you
Telling you all my dark secrets and fantasies
Telling you tales of places I once flew.

Oh love! I want to compose songs for you
Including lyrics of our conversation
Including drumming of our heartbeats too.

Oh love! I want to write odes for you

ENDLESS BEAUTY OF DIVINE

<u>UNNATI SAWANT</u>

She is a budding and bubbly writer expressing her creative mind in pen and ink. Born in city of dreams , passionate to travel round the world . Aspires to become CA and have a doctorate degree in Economic.

Book Benchers

Red seeks attention ;
Stimulates to be caution .
Orange signifies adventurous ;
Expresses freedom and dangerous.

Yellow is full of positivity ;
Awakes awareness to motivity .
Lime green denotes growth ;
Nurture us from our birth .

Kelly green represents stability ;
Encourages upto our ability.
Sky blue gives us wisdom ;
Inspires productivity to kingdom .

Royal blue symbolizes responsibility;
Creates impression and creativity .
Violet fantasizes imagination ;
Motivates action and communication.

Pink is playful and immature ;
Life is not so impure.
Brown needs all comforts ;
Suppress emotions and tells efforts .

Gray is quite quiet ;
Associate timeless and diet .
Black gives power and control ;
Endless Beauty rolls to decontrol.

RAJESHWARI PANDIAN

Raji pandian was a dark lover. She built up her strong feelings there. She wanna express her feelings through words, so started doing the anthologies as a co-author.

Instagram id - Raji pandian (Dreamer_24_ji)

Book Benchers

The morning wake up with eagerness to play in the
streets,
Imagining myself as the most stylish one,
After wearing my brother's old outfits!
Mom ties up my hair two high ponies,
Finishing the breakfast improperly,
Here our real game begins with the sun,
For the whole day he tries to defeat us,
Atlast the sun give up in the eve with a goodbye!
But we won't,
The part 2 begins with the stars and moon!
By watching the tv serials with ultimate interest,
Even I can't understand some dialogue as I was
below 18,
Thus, Our late evenings passes peacefully with my
family,
And the day ends with the stories of mother and
grandmother!
Nothing can beat the warmth besides our mother
while sleeping!
Yes that was the days when I slept without
depressions!

ANKUR MISHRA

बातें अपनी दिल की इस कदर किया करते हैं,
जज़्बात को बयां कोरे पन्ने मे किया करते हैं।

ये हैं अंकुर मिश्रा जो वर्तमान मे देवास मध्यप्रदेश मे
कार्यरत एक उभरते हुए लेखक हैं जो कि जिंदगी और
नौकरी का संतुलन बनाये रखते हुए अपने लेखन के शौक
को जिंदा रखे हुए हैं। इनकी रचनाये पच्चीस से ज्यादा ई-
बुक/किताबो मे प्रकाशित हो चुकी या होने वाली हैं।
भविष्य मे ये अपनी सभी रचनाओ को खुद की पुस्तक मे
संजोने का ख्वाब रखते हैं। इंस्टाग्राम मे आप इनसे अपने
विचार ankdip2801 मे साझा कर सकते हैं ।

<u>उस दिन का इंतजार</u>

जिस दिन से दोगे साथ मेरा तुम,
उस दिन से हर पसंद पूरी होगी ।

जिस दिन से बिन कहे समझोगे तुम,
उस दिन से कोई आस न अधूरी होगी ।

जिस दिन से रूठोगी मगर सिर्फ प्यार से,
उस दिन से रिश्तो मे जरा भी न दूरी होगी ।

जिस दिन से सच्चा दोस्त मानोगे मुझे तुम,
उस दिन से अपने बीच कोई न मजबूरी होगी ।

जिस दिन से उठायेंगे जिम्मा इकदूसरे का,
उस दिन से किसी तीसरे की न मजदूरी होगी ।

जिस दिन से पायेंगे इकदूसरे मे इत्मिनान दोनो,
उस दिन से रिशतों की महक फिर कस्तूरी होगी ।

पर जाने कब मुकम्ममल होगा उस दिन का इंतजार,
एकतरफा इश्क आखिर कब तक रहेगा यूं बेकरार ।

ये दौर असमंजस का

है क्यूं महज समझौता,ये दौर असमंजस का,
खत्म क्यू नही होता,ये दौर असमंजस का ।

फलसफा जिंदगी का,
है कुछ ऐसा उलझा हुआ,
जैसे कशमकश मे रह के भी मै,
सबकी नजर मे हुं सुलझा हुआ,
गलतफहमी मे गुम है,ये दौर असमंजस का,
खत्म क्यू नही होता,ये दौर असमंजस का,

धांधली के धंधे अब तो आम है,
मुखौटों मे छुपे हर चेहरे हैं,
उम्मीदो का रोज होता कत्लेआम है,
सबके मन मे छिपे राज बहुत गहरे हैं।
दुनिया मे कौन समझे,ये दौर असमंजस का,
खत्म क्यू नही होता,ये दौर असमंजस का।

RAVISHANKER NISHAD (ARVI)

यह रविशंकर निषाद है । ये शाखा :- तमनार, जिला :- रायगढ़ (छत्तीसगढ़) के निवासी हैं । इनका जन्म 19 जून 2000 में हुआ था ।। यह अभी इंजीनियरिंग कॉलेज में पढ़ाई कर रहे है । इनकी रुचि कविताएं लिखना है और यह किताबों के शौकीन भी है ।।

Instagram id - @arvinishad

आज फिर से उसका ख्याल आया

आज फिर से उसका ख्याल आया है
मेरे दिल की दरवाजे पर दस्तक जोरदार आया है
मैंने आहिस्ता आहिस्ता संभाला खुदको
देख तो किसी के प्यार का इश्तहार आया है ।।
मैंने नज़रों को उसकी तरफ घुमाकर देखा
मेरे लिए प्यारा सा फूलों का गुलदस्ता आया है
कोई अपने दिल का पैगाम मेरे लाया है
एक बार नहीं ये नज़राना बार बार आया है ।।
मैंने भी दिया जवाब भिजवाया मैंने भी गुलाब
देख कर उसे वो शरमाई मेरे पास दौड़ी चली आई
उसने कहा इश्क़ के आशियाने में मुझे जगह देदो
उसके लहराते बाल गुलाबी गाल
चमकती आखों में देख मुझे खुमार आया ।।
मैंने थामा उसका हाथ प्रिये
अब छोड़ुंगा ना कभी तेरा साथ ।।
हाथों में डाले हाथ उसे मैं
जिंदगी की हमसफ़र बना आया ।।।

मेरी ज़िन्दगी

ज़िंदगी की तलाश में खोया सा रहता था मैं
इधर उधर की ताक झांक से बेहतर सोया रहता मैं
मैं सपनों को जीने की कोशिश करता हूं
मेहनत कर खुदको तैयार करता हूं
ना जाने कब कैसे कहां मेरी मंजिल मुझसे मिलेगी
ना जाने कब मेरे मन की बगिया में खुशियों की फूल
खिलेगी ।
हर लम्हा उसके इंतजार का आलम रहता है ।
रसिया बिन तनहा जैसे उसका बालम रहता है ।
वफादारी,जिम्मेदारी और कर्तव्यनिष्ठा का भान है मुझे
जो भी हूं जैसा भी हूं अभिमान है मुझे ।।
मैं रहूं ना रहूं फर्क किसको पड़ता है यहां ।
दौलत के भूखे बसते है इंसान रहते हैं कहां ।
दुनियादारी से दूर अकेला मैं खुद में खुशहाल हूं ।
जिंदगी के साथ जीता हूं मैं भी कमाल हूं ।।

<u>S.SUGANTHI</u>

Suganthi has been writing for over two years. She provides philosophical writings. Her educational background in English literature has given her a broad base for writings. Her books are available in Amazon Kindle named Heartly Sayings and Healing journey-11

Instagram id - chum_moon

Book Benchers

Just words aren't enough to let someone
know how much you love them. You need to make
them
feel. How? Through your actions. Love can easily
be put
into words but to frame it into actions? Only the
ones
who actually truly love you, will act in the ways that
will
project love towards you. Many times we are unable
to
feel love from the other side because the truth is that
it
isn't there at all! The next time when someone says
they
love you, believe it in your heart when you see them
putting efforts to make you happy and feel lovable.

ENDLESS BEAUTY OF DIVINE

<u>DAKSHITA JAISWAL</u>

Dakshita jaiswal is a 18 year old Management student. She is from Gonda, Uttarpradesh. Being a voracious reader and writer, She has organized multiple events and itself is a poet, storyteller, blogger and a published author.

She is the core team member of Happy hearts organization, an event organizing house. She inculcates high interest into the field of writing and have performed at various platforms. You can search her on Instagram @invoicer_dakshita_jaiswal.

तुझको कविता कहूँ, या खुद को शायरा......!

नज़्मों में एक अश्क सा छोड़ा था,

अज्ञात दिशा में यू इश्क़ ने मोड़ा था,

जहाँ ज्ञात सैलाब में एक अज्ञात सा ख्वाब था,

दबी मुस्कुराहटों में उसकी छुअन का एहसास था,

जहाँ उसकी धड़कनों में धड़कते दिल का छिपा राज़ था,

ए ख़ुदा, ये इश्क और मुश्क में जाने कैसा शाज़ था,

जहाँ उसके लबों पर रूहानियत भरा , ऐतबार था,

इख़्तियार में उसकी चुप्पी में छुपा कुछ सार था,

कुछ लम्हों में यून इस क़दर उसमें बसा मेरा संसार था

सही या ग़लत , जाने यह इश्क़ का कैसा वार था,

न दरिया और ना ही दायरा ,

न ज़रिया और ना ही कायरा ,

तुझको कविता कहूँ , या खुद को शायरा!

PRAKHAR RAGHUWANSHI

I am Prakhar Raghuwanshi from betul city of madhya pradesh, currently studying in class 12th and 15 years old. I have been involved in writing works specially poetry since the last one year.

Instagram id - prkhrrghuwnshi_1

"ख्वाइश"

ऊंचा उड़ने की ख्वाइश जो है,
पतन को भी सहना पड़ेगा।
आगे बढ़ने की ख्वाइश जो है,
पीछे कभी तो रहना पड़ेगा।
दरिया लांघने की ख्वाइश जो है,
बहाव में भी बहना पड़ेगा।
जीत जाने की ख्वाइश जो है,
हार से तो लड़ना पड़ेगा।
मुकाम पाने की ख्वाइश जो है,
कठिन राहों से गुज़रना पड़ेगा।
ख्वाब देखने की ख्वाइश जो है,
सपने बुरे भी तो देखना पड़ेगा।

PRAKASH TURIYA (RAGHUWANSHI)

Prakash Turiya, Belonging from Chhindwara ,
Madhya Pradesh.
M.pharma, working as senior executive medical
writer

Instagram id - light@Raghuwanshi

<u>उसी से तो होता संसार हैं,</u>

वो करती सबसे प्यार है, उसी से तो होता संसार हैं।
कभी माँ की ममता में, तो कभी पत्नी के घूंघट में।
कभी बहन की खुशियों में, वो दिखता हर बार हैं।
उसी से तो होता संसार हैं।

वो हस्ती भी हैं, वो रोती भी हैं,
कुछ न कहकर, सब कुछ कहेति भी हैं।
उसकी डांट का असर कुछ होता इस कदर हैं।
उसके कंगन की खनक में दिल खोता इस कदर हैं।
उसी से तो होता संसार हैं,
उसी से तो होता संसार हैं।।।।।

ENDLESS BEAUTY OF DIVINE

NAVEEN BHARDWAJ

Myself Naveen bhardwaj a programmer by
profession a lover of poetry maker and like reading
books and audiobooks and he has telegram channel
@TheNBbook
Instagram id - na.vin7832

Your life has already many ups and down and you are telling I can't hold this pain . What you will do if you came back in your time your regret which you had before or instead try again and never give up on something because pain may be temporary but regret last forever.

Sometimes we think we putting lots of efforts in our work but the result still out of reach and we begin losing our enthusiasm and stop believing in ourself . We self doubt our inner potential that we are not worthy of that thing and starts blaming the society it's wrong mindset.

We all have different skill but some know their skill early and other waiting for that one sign to know their inner capability . The other person complement us and we start doing the same thing . We usually depended on our society, instead try to find out the best version of you.

TALIMA DAS

Talima Das is a student. She has interest in writing on social media platform. She is a co-author of 10+ anthologies.

Instagram id - 1talimadas

<u>QUOTES ON BEAUTY</u>

The eyes can show the beauty of heart. We should have a beautiful heart. And smile is the real beauty of face and heart. So smile always.

The love is beauty. The faith is beauty. The hope is beauty. The knowledge is beauty.

You can fall in love with a beautiful face. But you can't love an ugly heart. This is the relation between love and beauty.

ENDLESS BEAUTY OF DIVINE

KAARTHIKVEL V.S

A budding writer who loves to play with words
interested in story writing, poetry and lyric writing.
He had worked as co author in few anthologies and
written two album songs in Tamil and publishing
his quotes through his blog in Instagram

Instagram id - kavi_pithan05

<u>WILL YOU FORGIVE ME ?</u>

Are you ignoring me ?
Are you hating me ?
Are you avoiding me ?
Are you lying that you are busy?
What happened to you my love ?
Why are you making me to feel lonely ?
These many questions runs in my mind
The pain of your separation is makes me blind
I am unable to do my works
I am struggling day by day minute by minute
without you
Will you forgive me ? or will you forget me ?
Will you stay with me? Or will you leave me ?
I don't know what will you say
I will be waiting for you till my last day

ENDLESS BEAUTY OF DIVINE

GARGI GHOSH

A girl who lives in BERHAMPUR,
Murshidabad.she has completed her master's degree
in English literature
Writing is her passion.she wants to spread positive
vibe & Love at her society.

Instagram id - @bong girl gargi 12

<u>ENDLESS BEAUTY</u>

Your endless beauty
In your heart.
Your heart is most beautiful.
No beauty shines brighter
Than a good heart.
Beauty is not on face
Beauty is a light in the heart.
Your inner beauty
Never needs a make-up.
Outer beauty is just a gift.
Inner beauty is an accomplishment.
It's full of confidence
Determination & LOVE.

GARGI GHOSH

SHIVANG SHARMA

शिवांग शर्मा आज के युग के नए शायर हैं। शायर साहब वाराणसी के निकट स्थित मऊ जिले से आते हैं। इन्होंने कई पुस्तकों में सह - लेखक और संकलक के रूप में काम किया हैं। शायर साहब वर्तमान समय में राष्ट्रीय प्रौद्योगिकी संस्थान पटना से इंजीनियरिंग कर रहे हैं। इनके लिखने का सिलसिला क्यूँ शुरू हुआ ये आपको नीचे के लेख में दिखेगा -

" मिलता नहीं मुझे कोई
अकेला रहता हूँ मैं ,
लेता हूँ सहारा कलम का
पन्नों पे चीख देता हूँ मैं। "
Insta I'd -
@__dil_e_alfaaz__

बन के आईना दुनिया को
उसका असर चेहरा दिखाऊंगा,

क्या चीज़ हूँ
एक दिन ये सारे
जहान को दिखाऊंगा,

बहुत गुमान हैं
सुरज को आपकी तपिश पे,

जो अपनी तपिश पे आ जाऊँ तो
रातें भी रौशन कर जाउँगा।

ENDLESS BEAUTY OF DIVINE

<u>SRIJITA SAHA</u>

Co-author Srijita Saha is a good writer from Kolkata.She has completed her.education in 12th in science stream. She has been writing poetry for 2-3 months as her passion. She wants to be a writer in future.

Instagram id - feel_words_of_quoetry

<u>BEAUTY IN MIND</u>

One's mind should have the perfect beauty to judge
others,
Beauty is in you which makes you bother.
Beauty has power,
But never make anyone feel lower.
Beauty is in mind,
That every individual has to find.
Beauty is not just a word,
it's just like a flying bird.
Beauty is a feeling of mind,
That's everything must be kind.
Beauty is in your thought,
It's not easy to be bought.

YOGESH GURJAR CHINU

Her name is Yogesh Gurjar and nickname is Chinu, it is from Gautam Buddha Nagar district of Uttar Pradesh.

She loves to write and read thoughts, has written more than 1300 poems and quotes.

She has written as a co-author in 410 Anthology. Her first solo book is titled (सच्ची बातें "चीनू").

Instagram id - @yogeshgurjar369

<u>MOTHER'S LOVE</u>

This is not the magic of mother's anklets,
It is mother's love which is incalculable,

This mother's love is blind
Who wants more than her life even before coming
into the world,

This is the power of mother's love,
It is mother's love which comes out when the
mother gets hurt.

This is the best rites given by him.
This is his lad, this is his taught behavior,

The children leave the mother's love,
But the mother never leaves the side of the children,

Sometimes in the ashram, sometimes she dies on the
streets,
But she never gives a badass to her son,

Just look carefully, you understand carefully,
You will be able to live happily ever after by
hurting your mother..!!

ENDLESS BEAUTY OF DIVINE

PARENTS

There is no clap for closed luck,
There is no branch of happy hopes,

Parents' prayers never go empty
His bag is never empty for children,

Despite having a thousand difficulties, the one who
has always pushed us forward,
Even while falling, we have been taught to walk by
lifting,

Such is the shadow of our parents,
There is life's most precious Maya,

Hunger for wealth is bad...
It has broken so many houses,

Don't know how many relationships it has broken,
Many fools have also broken relations with their
parents for the sake of this,

There is darkness in every house without parents,
It's morning in the hut with parents too...!!

ANUSHA SATHIA

Anusha is a writer and a poet hailing from India. She is currently in high school. She has been writing since quite a few years and that has been her passion. She uses her positive attitude and tireless energy to encourage others to work hard and succeed and she writes because she enjoys expressing herself. For more of her work, please check out her Instagram handle: @_thelittletherapist

ENDLESS BEAUTY OF DIVINE

Is it hate
Or is it a thought
To not to think
about what keeps me awake!

What if one day
Lying on my bed
Or roaming in the woods
myself asks me
why didn't you wrote
on what made you this
who you are today

will I have any answer
or just a gesture
it was just to not
indulge with wounds anymore
if I can't heal a scare
I don't want to be a salt!

Will he get it
Will she understand it
Why six feet became a six inch
and high pitch a mumbler
a egoist girl lost self-esteem
an angry bird kept mum
and clinched her fist all day long!
with borrowed sorrow

* 9 7 8 9 3 9 1 4 2 3 7 8 0 *